Nothing's Gonna Stop Us Now
AND
The Hit Songs
OF
Diane Warren

VOLUME 1

In memory of my Father

I will always remember my Dad for his love and devotion to me. He was always there when I needed him which was quite often, and always there when anyone needed the love and support of a friend. In the early part of my career it was he who encouraged me and kept my spirits up during the all-too-many rejections I endured. I thank God that he was around to enjoy my success. I know he was proud. I pray that he's found peace. I will miss him terribly.

Diane

Cover Photo of Diane Warren: Cliff Watts

Foreword

For a songwriter there is no better feeling in the world than for someone to love their songs. And when they become successful it is a wonderful validation to know something you've done has touched somebody, made them feel something, made them laugh, made them cry, or maybe just made them dance.

This book represents some of the songs I feel especially close to these past few years. I would like to think of it as Volume One of many songbooks to come. I hope you enjoy the songs, they're for you.

With love,
Diane

CONTENTS

TITLE	ARTIST	PAGE
AND THE NIGHT STOOD STILL	Dion	76
BLAME IT ON THE RAIN	Milli Vanilli	134
DON'T TURN AROUND	Aswad	37
GIVE A LITTLE LOVE	Aswad	107
HOW CAN WE BE LOVERS	Michael Bolton	87
I DIDN'T WANT TO NEED YOU	Heart	123
I DON'T WANNA LIVE WITHOUT YOUR LOVE	Chicago	140
IF I COULD TURN BACK TIME	Cher	21
IF YOU ASKED ME TO	Patti La Belle	92
I GET WEAK	Belinda Carlisle	9
I'LL BE YOUR SHELTER	Taylor Dayne	63
JUST LIKE JESSE JAMES	Cher	116
LOOK AWAY	Chicago	27
LOVE WILL LEAD YOU BACK	Taylor Dayne	4
NOTHING'S GONNA STOP US NOW	Starship	51
RHYTHM OF THE NIGHT	De Barge	60
THE SAME LOVE	The Jets	56
THROUGH THE STORM	Aretha Franklin and Elton John	103
WALK AWAY	Michael Bolton	111
WE'RE NOT MAKING LOVE ANYMORE	Barbra Streisand	97
WHEN I SEE YOU SMILE	Bad English	42
WHEN I'M BACK ON MY FEET AGAIN	Michael Bolton	33
WHEN THE NIGHT COMES	Joe Cocker	68
WHEREVER WOULD I BE	Cheap Trick	130
WHO WILL YOU RUN TO	Heart	15
YOUR BABY NEVER LOOKED GOOD IN BLUE	Exposé	81

LOVE WILL LEAD YOU BACK

Words and Music by
DIANE WARREN

in my heart___ I know_____ oh,___ yeah.___ Love will lead you

Coda

___ back,___ oh,___ yeah.___ Love will lead___ you back,___ some-day I just

know___ that love will lead you back to my arms,___ it___ won't be long.___ One of these

days,___ oh, love will lead___ you___ back,___ ah._____

I GET WEAK

Words and Music by
DIANE WARREN

Moderate Rock

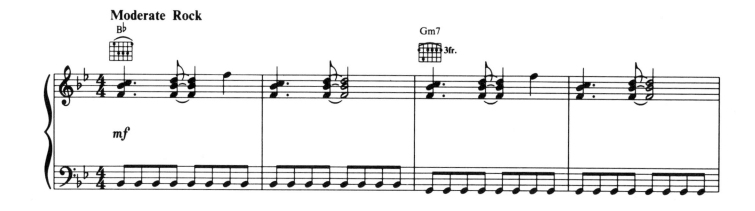

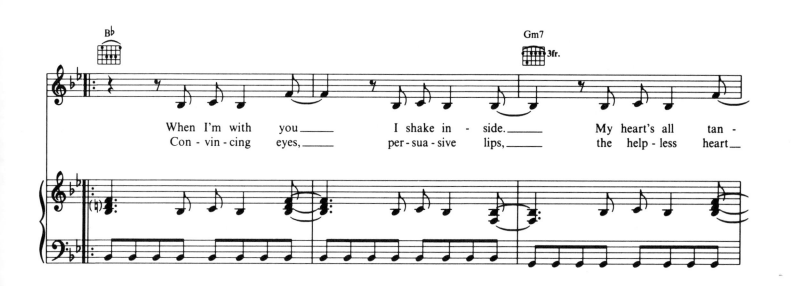

When I'm with you____ I shake in - side.____ My heart's all tan -
Con - vin - cing eyes,____ per - sua - sive lips,____ the help - less heart

WHO WILL YOU RUN TO

Medium Rock

Words and Music by
DIANE WARREN

You're not sure what you want to do with your life but you're sure of who you don't want in it.
You don't know what it's like to live on your own 'coz you've al-ways had me there be-side you.

a - way the tears you cry, ___ who's gon - na love ___ you, ba - by, as good as

To Coda

IF I COULD TURN BACK TIME

Words and Music by
DIANE WARREN

1.3. I did-n't real-ly mean to hurt you.
2. Too strong to tell you I was sor-ry.

I did-n't want to see you go. I know I made you cry,
Too proud to tell you I was wrong. I know that I was blind

but ba-by,
and dar-ling, if I could turn back time, if I could find

— a way, I'd take back those words that hurt

To Coda ⊕

LOOK AWAY

Words and Music by
DIANE WARREN

WHEN I'M BACK ON MY FEET AGAIN

Words and Music by
DIANE WARREN

DON'T TURN AROUND

Words and Music by
DIANE WARREN and ALBERT HAMMOND

WHEN I SEE YOU SMILE

Words and Music by
DIANE WARREN

When I see you smile, ____

1. ba - by, when I see you ___ smile at ___ me.

2. ba - by, when I see you smile ___ at me. Some-times ___ I wan-na

47

When I see you smile

I can face the world. __ Oh, _____ you know

I can do an-y-thing. __ When I

NOTHING'S GONNA STOP US NOW

Words and Music by
DIANE WARREN and ALBERT HAMMOND

Moderate Rock

Look - ing in your eyes I see a par - a - dise, this world
— so glad I found you, I'm not gon - na lose you, what ev -

— that I found is too good to be true. Stand - ing here be - side you, want
er it takes I will stay here with you. Take you to the good times, see

THE SAME LOVE

Words and Music by
DIANE WARREN

RHYTHM OF THE NIGHT

Words and Music by
DIANE WARREN

I'LL BE YOUR SHELTER

Words and Music by
DIANE WARREN

Moderate beat

When there's clouds hang-in' in your sky, and they're just not let-tin' an-y light in,
I got arms strong e-nough to hold you, get you through an-y-thing you go through,

Instrumental

and you feel like you'd like to give in, don't you give up so soon.
an-y-thing that you need, you know, it's on - ly a touch a way.

WHEN THE NIGHT COMES

Words and Music by
DIANE WARREN, JIM VALLANCE
and BRYAN ADAMS

74

wan-na be the one you run to, wan-na be the one you come to. I just

wan-na be there with some-one when the night comes. Just

put all our cares be-hind us, and go where they'll nev-er find us. I just

wan-na be there be-side you when the night comes, when the night comes.

AND THE NIGHT STOOD STILL

Words and Music by
DIANE WARREN

I still re-

YOUR BABY NEVER LOOKED GOOD IN BLUE

Words and Music by
DIANE WARREN

You should hear___ what they're say-ing a-bout you. You should see___ the way___ they

talk be-hind___ my back.___ They say that you've found an-oth-er___ and

HOW CAN WE BE LOVERS

Words and Music by
DIANE WARREN, MICHAEL BOLTON
and DESMOND CHILD

whoa, whoa, _____ it's a no-win sit-u-a-tion.
whoa, whoa, _____ got-ta stop this love from dy-ing.
How can we be lov-ers if we

can't be _____ friends?_ How can we start o-ver when the fight-ing nev-er ends?_ Ba-by,

how can we make love if we can't make a-mends?____ Tell me how can we be lov-ers if we

can't be, can't be friends?____

IF YOU ASKED ME TO

Words and Music by
DIANE WARREN

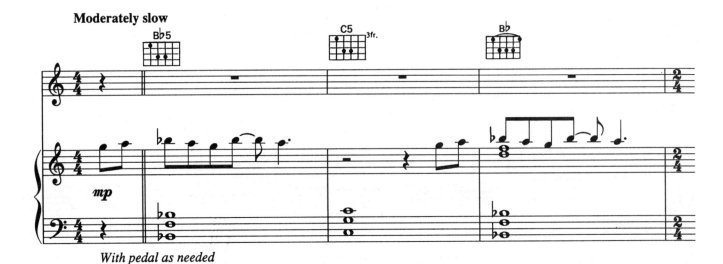

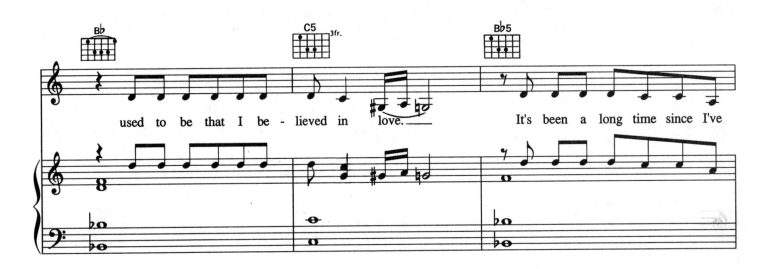

WE'RE NOT MAKING LOVE ANYMORE

Words and Music by
DIANE WARREN and MICHAEL BOLTON

THROUGH THE STORM

Words and Music by
DIANE WARREN and ALBERT HAMMOND

GIVE A LITTLE LOVE

Words and Music by
DIANE WARREN and ALBERT HAMMOND

WALK AWAY

Words and Music by
DIANE WARREN and MICHAEL BOLTON

JUST LIKE JESSE JAMES

Words and Music by
DIANE WARREN and DESMOND CHILD

119

To Coda

To- night you're gon- na go down in flames,___ just like Jes - se James.___

Instrumental solo

You think you'll knock me off my feet 'till I'm flat on the floor,___ 'til my

heart is cry- in' In- dian and I'm beg- gin' for more.___ So come on ba - by, come on ba - by,

I DIDN'T WANT TO NEED YOU

Words and Music by
DIANE WARREN

Moderate Rock

Ba - by,___ I nev - er gave___ my heart to an - y - one,___ oh,___ no.___ Used to think that love was a game.___ I used to make it

WHEREVER WOULD I BE

Words and Music by
DIANE WARREN

Moderate Rock Ballad

When my world is turn - ing, when it's turn - ing up - side down,___
When the dreams I dream,___ all seem a mil - lion miles a - way,___

when all I see is rain, when I think the night won't end,___
when I'm sure I'll nev - er win, when it's look - ing like I've lost my faith,___

BLAME IT ON THE RAIN

Words and Music by
DIANE WARREN

I DON'T WANNA
LIVE WITHOUT YOUR LOVE

Words and Music by
DIANE WARREN and ALBERT HAMMOND

Tempo I

through.

Now I know that I— ain't real-ly liv-ing if I have to live with-

out you. I don't wan-na live with-out— your love, I don't wan-na

face the night— a-lone.— I could nev-er make it through—my life if I had to

make it on— my own.— I don't wan-na love no-bod-y else, I don't wan-na

To Coda